Kids & Computers

The Internet

Charles A. Jortberg

Published by Abdo & Daughters, 4940 Viking Drive, Suite 622, Edina, Minnesota 55435.

Copyright © 1997 by Abdo Consulting Group, Inc., Pentagon Tower, P.O. Box 36036, Minneapolis, Minnesota 55435 USA. International copyrights reserved in all countries. No part of this book may be reproduced in any form without written permission from the publisher.

Printed in the United States.

Cover and Interior Photo credits: Wide World Photos
Archive Photos
Jortberg Associates

Edited by John Hamilton

Library of Congress Cataloging-In-Publication Data

Jortberg, Charles A.
The Internet / Charles A. Jortberg.
p. cm. -- (Kid and computers)
Includes index.
Summary: Discusses the history, development, capabilities, and uses of the massive communications system known as the Internet.
ISBN 1--56239-727-3
1. Internet (Computer network)--Juvenile literature. [1. Internet (Computer network)]
I. Title. II. Series: Jortberg, Charles A. Kids and computers.
TK5105.875.I57J7   1997
004.6 ' 7--dc20
                                                    96-32640
                                                       CIP
                                                        AC

About the Author

Charles A. Jortberg graduated from Bowdoin College in 1951 with a Bachelor's Degree in Economics. Mr. Jortberg joined IBM in 1954 and served in several capacities. Among his assignments were coordinating all of IBM's efforts with the Air Force, managing a 20-person team of IBM engineers, and directing a number of technical programs at NASA's Electronic Research Laboratory. He formed Jortberg Associates in 1972, where he currently works, to provide an outlet for his start-up technology experience.

Contents

The Internet

There are few times that you pick up a newspaper or watch a TV program where some reference to the "Internet" is not made. It seems as if every company and organization has its own "Web site." These terms are becoming part of our daily lives, and will continue to expand their influence. Let's examine what the Internet is and what the "World Wide Web" means, and then find out how it was created and why.

The Internet is a massive communications system that handles millions of messages passing every second among computers all over the world. This system allows you to call your friends' computers in any part of the country and leave messages for them. It also allows you to shop through catalogs of hundreds of companies that will show pictures of their products on your computer screen. When you see something you want, you can order it over the same computer connection.

Opposite page: A student surfing the Internet.

Bulletin Boards

All over the United States there are hundreds of groups that talk to each other on the Internet on a regular basis. Many of these people have never met except over the network, and yet they seem to be very old friends. One feature of the Internet is a bulletin board system where questions can be posted and read by millions of interested people.

Sometimes people have a problem that they need help solving. They ask the question on the Internet and millions of people can answer. In one case a man in New Jersey had a very rare medical problem in his family and none of the doctors in his hospital could help him. When he described the problem on an Internet bulletin board a doctor in California called him immediately and a cure was found. There are very few questions that are posted on these bulletin boards where somebody doesn't know the answer.

Julia Becker poses beside her home computer while
logged onto the CyberKids Home Page. CyberKids has
a bulletin board that allows young people to leave
messages for each other.

Internet Origins

For a good understanding of the Internet and what it can do for you, it is important to understand how the network got started. In February 1958 President Eisenhower and the rest of the United States were in shock as the Russians launched the first satellite, called *Sputnik*, into orbit. As *Sputnik* circled the globe, America became worried that it was losing its position as the world leader in science and technology. The president saw the need for a high-level organization that could direct the efforts of America's technology into new areas that would allow us to regain our position in the world.

It was decided that this new technology agency would be organized within the Department of Defense. This is the agency within the Federal Government that controls all of the armed services, including the Army, Navy, Air Force, and the Marine Corps. The new organization was named the Advanced Research Projects Agency. Like a lot of other groups, it had a shorter name formed from its first initials. The new agency became known as ARPA.

The major role of ARPA was to develop technical projects by granting money to organizations and scientists. ARPA was constantly looking for people who had new ideas, and for companies that could make the ideas work. The people who managed ARPA were convinced of the future need for expanding knowledge in the field of computers. If the U.S. was to leap forward in the technology race, ARPA was convinced it would happen because of improvements in computer technology. To help this along, a group was formed within ARPA that would advance computer science.

President Eisenhower (center) was helpful in starting ARPA, from which the Internet descended.

Several brilliant men headed up this computer group. Through them important developments received the money that was needed to make them work. Among these developments were timesharing at MIT, and the mouse invention created by Dr. Douglas Engelbart. By 1970 more than $26 million had been given by ARPA to computer projects.

In 1965 the director of the computer group became very concerned that the number of big computer installations in the U.S. were not able to communicate with each other. While it was true that the timesharing systems at the universities allowed people to communicate with the use of telephone lines, there was still no way for one big timesharing computer to talk with another by telephone lines. The management of ARPA agreed that if real progress was to continue, then the big machines should be able to talk with each other. This decision led to the creation of a large network of computers known as ARPANET.

The U.S. Air Force was one of the original
branches of the defense department to use
ARPANET, which eventually became the Internet.

ARPANET

The original design that was used for ARPANET had been devised at a time when the government was worried what would happen to communications in the U.S. if there was ever a nuclear attack. One of the important features of the original network was how reliable it was and how it could adjust to trouble. When the idea was first created, it relied on the fact that the network would be made up of several connected centers called "nodes."

A node is a place where messages come in and are then sent to their next stop on the way to the final destination. It's the same as if you were taking a car trip from Boston to Los Angeles. On the way you could take any one of several routes. You could go through Chicago, or Nashville, and then to St. Louis or Denver, and through other cities until you reached Los Angeles. On the ARPANET a message could also take one of several routes. With these many routes, if one was broken by an attack, an earthquake, or any disaster, then the message could be sent on a different path.

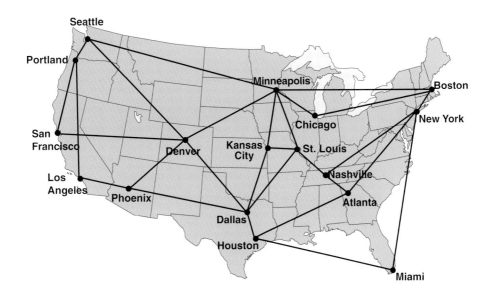

The ARPANET had many connecting centers. If one link was broken, a message could be sent along a different path.

A strength of the ARPANET was the fact that it did not depend on one strong central computer, but instead relied on several connected locations. This allowed continued operation if there was a problem in any one location. The same rules have been built into the Internet, and so it too is very reliable and not likely to fail. By 1969 ARPANET had its first three locations up and running. There was no way that these pioneers could have known how widespread the use of this approach would become with the use of the Internet in the 1990s.

Computer Conferencing

In the beginning, ARPANET was to be used only among computers that were working on government projects. If one university was developing something, others could use it. It was easy to transfer this information over the network. Many of the original designers of ARPANET found that it was very easy to share their ideas by having conferences where one computer would talk to another. This became known as computer conferencing. Soon these users started using the network to converse with each other and to leave messages that could be picked up later by someone on the network. As new systems were developed, the spread of this information led to developments by others in the same fields.

As the number of users expanded, it didn't take long to figure out that what started as a system designed for one computer to talk to another turned out to be very useful for personal messages. Once the network was up and running, with

Weather technology uses computer conferencing
to share weather information around the world.

computers speaking to each other, the transfer of all types of data became very easy. Although the mission of ARPANET was to share information among government agencies and contractors, it didn't take long for the idea of leaving messages for people to become very popular.

While ARPANET was continuing to grow, many users of the early personal computers were finding that they could communicate with their systems. They found that with a modem they could use standard telephones to communicate with other users. A modem is a device that on one end converts computer signals to a form that can travel over telephone lines. On the other end, another modem converts the telephone signals back to computer signals.

E-mail

From these early experiments in the ARPANET and individual computers, users found that they could now leave messages for others in what became known as electronic bulletin boards. On these bulletin boards, you could send a special type of message that was not addressed to any one person, but would be available for anyone on the network to read. These bulletin boards are one of the main uses of the Internet today. It wasn't long before these users were setting up their own addresses so people could contact their computer directly or leave messages for them. By leaving messages like this, they were actually using a form of electronic mail, or "E-mail," as it is known by a lot of people.

By the end of the 1980s, there was so much interest in the use of a nationwide network it was clear that the older ARPANET could not handle the increases in the number of customers. It was also clear that the restrictions of ARPANET for government-related use was no longer as important as providing open access to a nationwide communications system. Today's Internet really got its push when President George

Bush signed into law the High Performance Computer/National Education Network. The government then approved the spending of nearly a billion dollars on projects that would help the creation of the nationwide network.

A teacher works with a student at the computer as part of the Education Network.

Fiber Optics

The result of this government investment is a nationwide network of very fast communications links capable of transmitting millions of messages every minute through a group of nodes that are spread throughout the country. The key to this blazing speed is the use of miles of fiber optic cable. Fiber optic cables are made of thousands of tiny strands of glass that look like wires wrapped into a bundle. Instead of cables made from strands of copper wire, glass strands carry the communications signals. Instead of electricity passing through the wires, the fiber optic cables transmit by passing light through the glass strands. The fibers are much smaller than in the copper wire, and also much, much faster. The electrical signals from one computer are converted into short bursts of light that travel through the glass fibers to their destination, where they are then converted back to computer signals.

By the middle of the 1980s it was obvious that the use of a nationwide network should continue to expand. During this time another agency of the U.S. government was also very concerned with the use of networks like the ARPANET.

Fiber optics helped to speed up the Internet.

The National Science Foundation, commonly called the "NSF," is an organization that provides government money to individuals and companies for research in various scientific areas. They started a network called the "NSFNET," which was to connect several huge computers and their users together.

The transmission lines now operating at millions of messages per minute was used by the NSFNET and the ARPANET. The entire operation became one INTERNET under the control of NSF in 1990, and ARPANET ceased to exist. Today the Internet receives the majority of its funding through government grants.

How Do You Use the Internet?

When you decide you want to become a user of the Internet, the best thing to do is to buy a book at your local computer store that will tell you what you will need on your computer to become a user. A PC with a modem is the basic requirement. If you want to be able to print out messages, a printer is also a good idea.

The next thing you want to do is to sign up with one of several companies that will arrange for you to connect to the Internet through a local phone number. This is a good idea because if you had to dial one of the long distance nodes it would be expensive. These companies will charge a fee for this connection. Sometimes the amount changes every month, depending on how much time you spend on the network. Other

companies charge the same amount each month no matter how much time you use. For the basic use of the Internet there are no additional charges, although when you use certain services offered by some faraway companies there can be additional costs.

One of the first things the local company will give you is your own Internet address. This is usually a collection of letters and numbers that end with the letters "com." Once you have your address, you can start using the Internet, usually called just the "net." The most popular use is electronic mail services that let you send messages to any location on the Internet system. You do this by using an address with your message telling the Internet where you want the message to go. With this mail service you can send the same message to hundreds of users if you make up a mailing list. For instance, you could make up a mailing list of all your relatives and friends that have computers and are on the net, and send one message out to all of them. With this service you also have an electronic "mailbox" where people can leave messages for you.

Opposite page: Young people on the Internet.

The Web

In addition to electronic mail, the most popular use of the Internet today is through the use of "Web sites."

In hundreds of locations all over the world, people and companies have set up their own networks or mini-networks. They have written programs and provided displays that show all the information and things that can be done at that location.

Each one of these Web sites has its own Internet address. When you call one of these addresses you are connected to that portion of the Web or small network.

Once you are connected, your screen will have a list of things you can do and see at that site. This is called a "menu," and is much like a table of contents in a book. If you take your mouse and click on one of the items it will open up that area and display the things you want to look at.

Many of these locations include pictures as well as written descriptions. Television networks might have a Web site that you can access for a number of reasons. When you reach them you might be given a choice of looking at this week's program schedule, or you might want to know about any specials that are

Chris Hemmings scrolls through Virtual World, an electronic magazine that can be read on the World Wide Web.

coming soon. A screen might show you the choices and you would click your mouse at the proper place and your answers would then be displayed.

There are hundreds of Web sites being added every day for countless different reasons, ranging from medicine to politics to sports. There are even sites where you can "browse" and see a listing of Web sites you might want to look at.

Thousands of companies and big organizations have Web sites on what is known as the "World Wide Web." This is a collection of thousands of smaller Web sites available to users by using their addresses that start with "WWW."

On the World Wide Web, thousands of companies and individuals have set up their own Web sites. One of the interesting uses is the chance to obtain free programs for your PC.

A number of locations offer some interesting things you can do with your computer, and will even send these programs to your computer over the telephone lines. Other companies offer advice on colleges and how to best prepare for certain careers.

Many companies who supply video games and other products offer an Internet location where you can ask questions or report trouble.

Because the Internet can be so much fun and informative, it can become a habit that costs a lot of money.

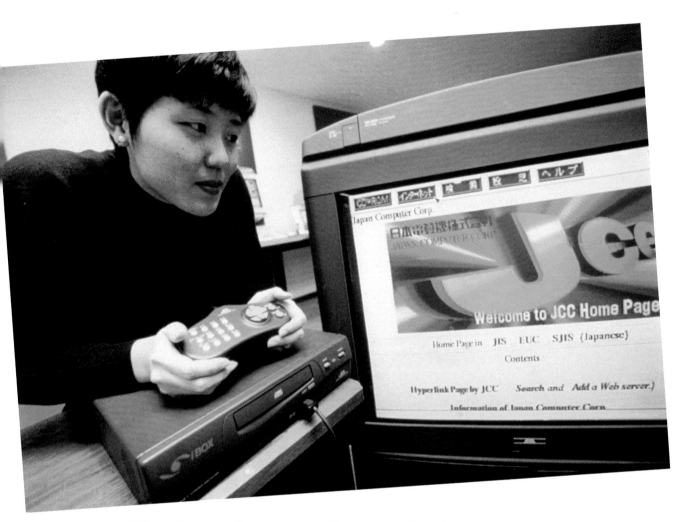

The Japan Computer Corporation home page.

Remember that the company that provides your connection may be charging you by the amount of time you spend on the Internet.

Cool Internet Sites for Kids

Broccoli Town

http://www.broccoli.com

Broccoli Town is an interactive Web site developed by Mann Packing Co. in Salinas, California. You can browse through a fictional town and learn just about everything you ever wanted to know about broccoli, including recipes and trivia. More interesting is a virtual tour that shows how broccoli is planted, processed, and shipped. The site also includes information on health and nutrition, plus interactive games and animation.

Eddie the Eco-Dog

www.mbnet.mb.ca/eddy

Eddie the Eco-Dog is a 7-foot-tall dog that rides a surfboard through outer space. No, really! This quirky site takes kids on a series of adventures, helping them learn about science and the environment. The creator of the site is a graphic designer who wanted to help young people learn about ecology.

Faces

www.web-usa.com/faces/

Faces is a hilarious Web site that works like one of those split-page children's books, except here all the face parts are from celebrities. Have some weird fun combining Michael Jackson's hair with Madonna's eyes and Winona Ryder's mouth. A good site when you need a quick laugh.

Family Internet

www.familyinternet.com

Family Internet is a large collection of information, arranged as a series of frames that makes it easy to find what you're looking for. The service includes such things as travel information, family health, and the Pet Corner, which is written by a board-certified veterinarian. Each section is like a separate information service. There's a lot of stuff here, more than you can browse in a single sitting. Definitely a Web page to bookmark on your favorite sites list.

KidPub
http://www.en-garde.com/kidpub/

KidPub is a Web site where young writers can publish their stories and interact with other authors. Started by a technical  writer in Boston as a way to encourage his 9-year-old daughter to write, KidPub is designed as an outlet for young writers to share their creativity and get feedback on their work. After submitting your story, you should see it posted in just a few days for the rest of the world to read. At the bottom of each story is a counter showing how many times your work has been read since it was posted, along with interesting statistics on who is reading it.

Kid's Window
http://jw.stanford.edu/KIDS/kids_home.html

Go to this award-winning World Wide Web site to learn all kinds of facts about Japanese culture. You'll find lively information on traditional Japanese food, including noodles, sushi, and rice dishes. Read Japanese folk tales, or browse current news stories related to Japan. Also included are instructions on arts & crafts, plus Japanese language classes, including a Japanese picture dictionary.

NASA Home Page

http://www.nasa.gov/

This is the official Web site of the National Aeronautics and Space Administration (NASA). Here you'll find lots of photos and information about the U.S. space program, including history, current Space Shuttle missions, and images from various space missions, including the Hubble Space Telescope.

Old-Time Radio

http://www.aic-radio.com

This site, developed by a company called Adventures in Cassettes, has listings of hundreds of old-time radio shows. Created to serve as an online catalog for the company, it's fun to browse through the lists and download digital sound bites. Some of the programs you can sample include snippets from "The Green Hornet," "War of the Worlds," "Sherlock Holmes," "Jack Benny," and many more.

The Ultimate Camera Page
http://www.cybercomm.net/~szymon/cam/new.html

A Web cam is a Web site connected to a video camera. The camera captures whatever it's pointed at and updates the still image every few seconds or minutes. The Ultimate Camera Page is a collection of Web cam sites, conveniently arranged by country. So far the site has links to 145 different Web cams, 52 outside the United States. Care to see what's going on at Mawson Station in Antarctica? Click the hypertext link to be instantly transported to a scene of snow and ice. Or watch the Valimaa crossing point between the Finland/Russia border. Or check out the progress of a new telescope being built atop Mauna Kea in Hawaii.

Virtual Frog Dissection Kit
http://george.lbl.gov/vfrog/

Ever want to cut into a frog and see what makes it tick, but were too squeamish to try? Or perhaps you think the whole idea of dissecting another creature is too cruel. If so, then this clever site is for you. The Virtual Frog Dissection Kit is an interactive program that lets you peek inside a frog layer by layer, without ever getting a drop of formaldehyde on your hands. Part of the "Whole Frog" project from the Lawrence Berkeley National Laboratory, the program lets you dissect a virtual frog, from the skin right down to the bones. It supports several languages, and includes the capability to make on-the-fly movies.

Virtual Museum of Computing
http://www.comlab.ox.ac.uk/archive/other/museums/
computing.html

On the Virtual Museum of Computing Web site, you can learn about the history of computing and explore online exhibits. This virtual museum includes a diverse collection of Web hyperlinks related to the history of computing and online computer-based exhibits available both locally and around the world. Some of the galleries include general historical information, computer-related museums, computer simulators, and Websites devoted to exploring the future of computing.

The White House For Kids
www.whitehouse.gov/WH/kids/html/kidshome.html

Check out the White House in Washington, D.C. This virtual tour, complete with history and interesting facts about the White House and the presidency, is hosted by a cartoon of Socks, President Clinton's cat.

Yahooligans!
http://www.yahooligans.com

Yahooligans! is a searchable, browseable index of the Internet designed for Web surfers ages 8 to 14. Using this kid-oriented search engine, specify a search word or set of words, and Yahooligans! will search its entire database to find listings that match the search words you provide. You'll find a search form or search button at the top of every Yahooligans! directory page. Yahooligans! will search titles, Web addresses, and comments to find listings that contain all of your search words. The site also has a "Cool" button that displays Web sites they think are cool. These sites may be entertaining, funny, wild, educational— and useful.

Glossary

Advanced Research Projects Agency (ARPA) - An agency within the Federal Government that was founded to advance technical research in the United States.

ARPANET - Network of large computers established by ARPA.

COM - Internet address usually has these three letters at the end. This address is given to users by their local connection company.

computer conferencing - One or more computers talking to another.

Department of Defense - A cabinet-level department of the U.S. government that controls the Armed Services.

electronic mail (E-mail) - Messages sent to and stored in computer memory.

electronic bulletin boards - A place to leave messages from one computer to another.

fiber optic cable - A cable made of tiny strands of glass.

High Performance Computer/National Education Network - An act President Bush signed into law which provided funds to help the creation of the nationwide network.

menu - Table of contents or selections. In computers the menu is usually shown on a computer display.

modem - A device that converts computer signals to a form that can travel over telephone lines, and also converts phone signals to computer signals.

mouse - Hand-held device that moves a cursor or pointer on the screen of a computer display.

National Science Foundation (NSF) - A Federal Government agency that provides money for scientific research.

node - A place where messages come and go on their way to a final destination.

NSFNET - National Science Foundation Network, which connects several large computer users together.

Sputnik - The Russian satellite that was the first ever into space.

website - Network or mini network.

World Wide Web (WWW) - A worldwide collection of websites that can be connected with one address.

Index

M

mailbox 23
mailing list 23
medical 6
menu 24
MIT 10
modem 16, 21
mouse 10, 24, 26

N

Nashville (TN) 12
National Science Foundation 20
Navy, U.S. 8
network 6, 8, 10, 12, 14, 17, 18,
    19, 21, 24
New Jersey 6
newspapers 4
nodes 12, 19, 21
NSFNET 20
nuclear attack 12

P

personal computers 16
politics 26
printer 21

R

Russians 8

S

science 8, 9, 20, 29
shopping 4
sports 26
Sputnik 8

T

technology 8, 9
telephone 10, 16, 26
television 4, 24
timesharing 10

U

United States 6, 8, 32

V

video games 26

W

Web sites 24, 26, 35
World Wide Web 4, 26, 30